STRENGTH
TO
STAND

Jennie L. Newbrough, D. Min.

Printed in the United States of America

©2015
All rights reserved

ISBN 978-1-60920-109-8

API
Ajoyin Publishing, Inc.
P.O. 342
Three Rivers, MI 49093
www.ajoyin.com

No part of this book may be reproduced or transmitted in any form or by any means, electronic or mechanical—including photocopying, recording, or by any information storage and retrieval system—without permission in writing from the publisher, except as provided by United States of America copyright law.

Please direct your inquiries to admin@ajoyin.com

CONTENTS

ix WELCOME

1 DAY 1
Take Your Stand

4 DAY 2
The Mystery

7 DAY 3
My Hero

10 DAY 4
Heart Song

13 DAY 5
God Is Not a Man

16 DAY 6
For Good

19 DAY 7
Maturity

22 DAY 8
Hold Tight

25 DAY 9
Same Power

28 DAY 10
As One

31 DAY 11
Like Israel

34 DAY 12
Loved

37 DAY 13
Essence

40 DAY 14
Most Blessed

43 DAY 15
Deny Self

46 DAY 16
P-U-S-H

49 DAY 17
Pressed

52 DAY 18
Scary as Hell

55	DAY 19 **King of Glory**	73	DAY 25 **Just Suppose**
58	DAY 20 **Look Up**	76	DAY 26 **Decided**
61	DAY 21 **Badge of Honor**	79	DAY 27 **Kingdom against Kingdom**
64	DAY 22 **Cover and Carry**	82	DAY 28 **Destiny**
67	DAY 23 **Hard Hearts**	85	DAY 29 **I Know**
70	DAY 24 **Rock Formation**	88	DAY 30 **Satisfied**

91 ACCESSING SONGS USED IN THIS DEVOTIONAL

WELCOME

To a time of Devotion that I pray will impact you as it has me.

In the summer of 2014 my pastor took a three month sabbatical. At the end of the time, he sent out an email saying he had read several books and that of all the books he recommended one, The Insanity of God, by Nik Ripken. Because I respect my pastor I immediately bought the book and read it. It broke my heart in all the right places, in all the right ways, at exactly the right time. I saw God's heart and understood the times in which we are living from a Biblical perspective as I never fully had before.

A few years prior, I was leading a tour in Israel and as our tour bus drove from the airport to Jerusalem the driver stopped at the top of a hill overlooking the old city of Jerusalem. We departed the bus to enjoy the scene and immediately I began to travail. I could hear the heart of Christ as He, too, overlooked the city and cried out . . . **"Oh, Jerusalem, Jerusalem, the one who kills the prophets and stones those sent to her! How often I wanted to gather your children together as a hen gathers her chicks under her wings, but you were not willing"** (Matthew 23:37).

I hear this same cry over Israel, the Church and our world today. Our Savior is crying for us to awaken to the times we are in and prepare our hearts to be who He has created us to be, **"for such a time as this"** (Esther 4:13).

It is our time to receive His . . .

STRENGTH TO STAND.

I pray that God will commune with you

throughout these Devotions and that

you will never be the same!

Jennie L. Newbrough, D. Min.

*"having done all to **STAND** . . . **STAND** . . ."*

Ephesians 6:13.

Day 1

TAKE YOUR STAND

Ephesians 6:13–14
*". . . and having done all to **stand**, **stand** . . ."*

There is a posture that God calls us to.
That posture is **standing**
Our **stand** is actually our heart position before God.
We **stand** in many ways and places for ourselves and for others.

When we take our **stand** we are to **stand fast**. We are to be unmoving, faithful, fixed, unwavering and committed. God calls us to take our place, **stand** and remain faithful to the end for we know in Whom we believe.

*"Watch, **stand fast** in the faith,
be brave, be strong . . ."*
(1Corinthians 16:13).

When we **stand** we also are to raise a **standard**. We lift up what we **stand** for. We lift up that in which we believe, have faith, hope and trust. This stand becomes a banner, a light, an example, a strong tower that others can rally to.
We **stand** in partnership with God.
*"Set up the **standard** toward Zion"* (Jeremiah 4:6).

You are called in Christ to be a **standard** bearer.

Raise high the Cross of Christ Jesus!

Day 1

The good news is that we do not **stand** on our own.

Christ is our **strength**!

Ephesians 6 reveals that we **stand** in Christ who is our belt of truth, our breastplate of righteous, our shield of faith, our helmet of salvation with the sword of the Spirit of the Word. We are able to **Stand** because . . .

It Is In Christ We **STAND!**

Let the righteousness of Christ be displayed through your life.
Be the **standard** bearer of His Kingdom before the world.

When life presses you, God gives you the Grace to
STAND.
By His Grace, in partnership with Christ, you can
STAND.
No matter what the circumstances . . .

In Christ
STAND!

Day 1

STRENGTH Fixed, immovable in Christ . . .
Does that describe you?
His Kingdom comes on earth as it is in heaven

As you **STAND** faithful . . . believing.
Having done all . . . **STAND!**

Day 2

THE MYSTERY

Colossians 1:27

". . . the glory of the mystery among the Gentiles; which is Christ in you, the hope of glory."

Even God calls it a mystery, so do not be troubled that you do not fully grasp it. But do embrace the amazing truth that Christ lives in you. By the power and work of the Holy Spirit Christ lives in you. It is not by your doing but by God's power that Christ lives in you. When you received Christ as your Savior you gave Him permission to live in you by the power of His Spirit.

Christ in you.
Think about that.
Christ In You!

Love, Joy, Peace, Patience, Kindness, Goodness,
Faithfulness, Gentleness, Self-control

In You!

Yes, all that is Christ is in you.
And Christ looks forward to living through you each and every day in each and every situation. He is glorified when you let Him live through you.

When you are Patient instead of frustrated, He is glorified. When you resist sin because His Self-control is in you He celebrates. When you

Day 2

resist the temptation to quit because His Faithfulness rises up in you He rejoices. When you bless your enemy with Kindness He is revealed in your Love. When you choose to forgive His Peace overcomes evil and His Goodness is made known.

Christ In You!
Christ delights in living through you.
His Kingdom comes on earth as it is in heaven through you!
You reveal His glory on earth.

Very humbly, the Apostle Paul says in Galatians 2:20 . . .

"It is no longer I who live, but Christ who lives in me . . ."

As Paul, may we humble ourselves.
Give Him Glory! Let Him live Big In You!

Day 2

STRENGTH   Choose day by day . . .
Circumstance by circumstance . . .
"No longer I, . . . but Christ."

STAND   Christ In You!

STAND   He is Glorified!

DAY 3

MY HERO

John 15:20
"If they persecuted me they also will persecute you . . ."

Christ made many promises to those who followed Him, however this is one promise we would prefer not to receive.

Are you prepared for persecution?

I have been very challenged by the story of Dmitri. Dmitri was honored to be persecuted for the sake of the Kingdom of God in Russia during the late 1970's. This is in my lifetime.

Most Russian churches were closed under the Communist Regime so God lead Dmitri and his family to study the Bible and worship in their own home. Soon neighbors came as well. When the authorities found out, Dmitri and his wife lost their jobs, their children were then expelled from school and finally Dmitri was thrown in prison. In prison he was the only believer among 1500 criminals.

Each morning in prison Dmitri would do what his father, years earlier, had taught him to do. Dmitri would **stand,** raise his hands and sing his "heart song" to God. The other prisoners would mock him and the guards would beat him, yet faithfully each morning Dmitri would **stand** and sing his "heart song" to God. Dmitri did grow weary of the beatings, yet faithfully, every morning for 17 years of imprisonment, Dmitri **stood** and sang to God. Then the fateful morning came when the guards arrived to take Dmitri from his cell for his execution.

Day 3

As he was lead through the prison, the 1500 prisoners who had mercilessly mocked his faith daily for 17 years **stood** and began to sing Dmitri's "heart song". The presence of God was mighty and, in terror, the guards released their hold on Dmitri and stepped away. Soon after, Dmitri was released from prison and returned to his family.

As I read Dmitri's true story in the book, *"The Insanity of God"* by Nik Ripken, I wept and immediately knew I had to find my "heart song".

I had to have the **Strength to Stand**, just as Dmitri did.

I now have my song . . .

What about you?

Do you know your "heart song"?

Day 3

STRENGTH   Ask God to reveal to you the song of worship that speaks to your spirit and gives you

Strength To Stand

God knows you and knows what song is your "heart song". God wants to prepare you for battle and enable you each day to Sing your Heart Song . . . be prepared . . .

STAND   No matter the . . .
Persecution, challenge, battle, opposition . . .

STAND   . . . **Sing!**

(Thank you, Pastor Steve Cordle
for encouraging Crossroads Church to read this inspiring book,
The Insanity of God by Nik Ripken.)

DAY 4

HEART SONG

2 Corinthians 12:9–10

"My grace is sufficient for you for my power is made perfect in weakness . . . For the sake of Christ, then, I am content with weaknesses, insults, hardships, persecutions, and calamities. For when I am weak, then I am strong."

The Apostle Paul wrote the above thoughts when he had learned to **STAND.** I am learning . . .

My "heart song" is **Outrageous Grace** by Godfrey Birtill.

I remember the first time I heard this life-giving song. I was with fellow Believers from over 100 nations at an Aglow International Conference. This song became imbedded in my heart, my mind, my spirit . . . over and over I would hear these wonderful words . . .

There's a whole lot of pain
But a lot more healing
There's a lot of trouble
But a lot more peace
There's a lot of hate
But a lot more loving
There's a lot of sin
But a lot more grace!

Day 4

Oh Outrageous Grace
Oh Outrageous Grace
Love unfurled by heavens hand
Oh Outrageous Grace
Oh Outrageous Grace
Through my Jesus I can stand!

There is a lot of fear
But a lot more freedom
There's a lot of darkness
But a lot more light
There's a lot of cloud
But a lot more vision
There is a lot of perishing
But a lot more Life!

There is an enemy
That seeks to kill what it can't control
It twists and turns
Making mountains out of molehills
But I will call on the Lord
Who is worthy of praise
I run to Him and I am saved!

Oh Outrageous Grace
Oh Outrageous Grace
Through my Jesus I can stand!

Day 4

STRENGTH   Read the lyrics slowly
Take time to listen to the words as you read.
It is real! It is truth!
Through your Jesus you can **STAND**!

STAND   In your weakness He is strong!

STAND   Embrace His **Outrageous Grace!**

(Thank you, Godfrey Birtill for for all of your heartfelt music but especially for,"Outrageous Grace"!)

Day 5

GOD IS NOT A MAN

Numbers 23:19

*". . . God is not a man, that He should lie,
Nor a son of man, that He should repent.
Has He said, and will He not do it?
Or has He spoken and, will not make it good?"*

In the early years of our marriage, my husband and I played a silent game. I seemed to always put jar lids on crooked. When my husband would find one he would, without a word, leave the jar on the counter for me to "get it right". I truly felt he had a problem.

One day I was teaching at a retreat on the subject of having a correct concept of God and the Holy Spirit brought the image of my peanut butter jar to my mind. Immediately, by the Spirit, I could see what I had never seen with my natural eyes or through my husband's attempts to help. I realized that when my lid was crooked air would get in to contaminate and spoil the purity of my peanut butter! Likewise, when our spiritual lids are on crooked the prince of the air invades our mind and spoils our concept of God. Satan looks for access.

**Having a true concept of God,
seeing God as He truly is, is essential
to having a right relationship with Him.**

God is not the one who rejected you, abused you, or lied to you.
He will not betray you, neglected you, or indulged you.
God is not the parent who was never there.

Day 5

Nor the one who gave you things but not himself.
He is not the one who called you hurtful names.
Nor the one who said you would never amount to anything.
God is not the one who said he would call and never did.
God is not the one whose love is conditional.
Nor the one who promised and failed.
God has not withheld acceptance or approval.
God will never leave you for another.

When we make God in the image of man, it distorts our relationship with Him.
We either fear Him and remain distant.
Or we strive through religion and works to earn His love.
Or we take Him for granted, disregard His holiness,
And believe He is our servant.

God does not have a human nature.
He will not relate to us as man does.
His ways are far above our ways.
We bear His image; He does not bear ours.

Day 5

STRENGTH   May the Holy Spirit free you from any wrong concept of God.
May the Spirit of Truth set you free to know God as He truly is.

STAND   Knowing . . .
Man may love . . . but God IS love.
Man may care . . . but God IS the Father of Compassion
Man may give . . . but God GAVE His own life for you

STAND   Knowing . . . God is NOT a man

Day 6

FOR GOOD

Genesis 45:5, 50:20

*"God sent me before you to preserve life . . .
you meant evil against me;
God meant it for good . . . to save many . . ."*

When was the last time you gloried in tribulation?
Jesus said we would have tribulations, that life would press us.
When life presses, who we truly are comes forth.
At the end of his story, Joseph, son of Jacob and the most
Christ-like man to live, said,
"God meant it for good . . ." Genesis 50:20.
What was meant for good?
The answer was Joseph's tribulation.

Joseph was called to bring God's salvation to his world just as we are each called to bring the salvation of Christ to our world. As soon as Joseph shared what God had revealed to him, his tribulation began. His angry envious brothers plotted to murder him, put him in a pit, and sold him into slavery. This favored son was now a servant. Joseph then chose righteousness and resisted seduction but was rewarded with false accusation and imprisonment. The chosen savior was now a prisoner. Things went from bad to worse for Joseph, all while he did right.

The Bible reveals that throughout Joseph's tribulation God's favor was with him. God was fully faithful. As a slave in Potiphar's house, Joseph prospered in all he did and was promoted to overseer. While in prison he was given authority over all the other prisoners.

Day 6

> In his tribulation, Joseph remained faithful and obedient.
> Pharaoh then appointed Joseph ruler second only to himself.
> Now the ultimate test, how would Joseph relate to others when he
> had power and position?

Through his 13 years of tribulation, God formed the character of Christ in Joseph. Famine came upon the land and the very brothers who had betrayed Joseph came to Egypt in need of mercy, having no idea Joseph was in a position of authority there

Joseph administered Kingdom authority with the character of his God. With mercy and compassion, forgiveness and grace, Joseph proclaimed to his brothers,

> *". . . you meant evil against me; God meant it for good"*

> As you endure the tribulations of life,
> the character of Christ is also
> being formed in you.
> You are the hope of your world, just as Joseph was for his.
> God will use you to be merciful and bring salvation.
> He will establish His Kingdom on earth as it is in heaven
> through you.

Day 6

STRENGTH God entrusts His authority to those who let the tribulations of this world work the character of Christ in them.

STAND Under pressure your character is being formed.

STAND God means it for GOOD!

DAY 7

MATURITY

Genesis 48:20
"May God make you as Ephraim and as Manasseh!"

This blessing from Jacob to Joseph's sons was significant and repeated as often in the early days of the people of Israel as the Lord's Prayer is for the people of God today. This blessing is as important for God's people today as it was for the people of God then.

Joseph named his firstborn son, *Manasseh* which means,
"for God has made me forget all my toil and all my father's house.
Joseph named his second son, *Ephraim* which means
"for God has caused me to be fruitful in the land of my affliction"
(Genesis 41:51–52).

In naming his firstborn, Manasseh, Joseph was choosing to let go of the pain of his past. Then when his second son, Ephraim, was born Joseph could embrace his future and be fruitful. The past was not hindering his future. He had let go. Is there something from the past you should let go of?

When Jacob blessed his grandsons he was prophesying and saying that the future would be greater than the past. We must each recognize this truth and be willing to look forward rather than become stuck in the past. In letting go of the past we are accepting what we cannot change and believing for new life.

Day 7

> It is easy to become stuck in the past with
> disappointment and resentment.
> However, we will not have the **Strength to Stand** in the present
> if we let the past pull us backwards..
> We must be fully present and believing for the future to be
> fruitful today and tomorrow.

Jacob was breaking tradition when he gave the first blessing, the double portion, to the second son. The normal pattern of inheritance was that the first born would inherit the greater portion. God was revealing that He will free us from our negative past and that our future can be fruitful.

> We know we have moved into maturity when
> we can embrace what is,
> make the most of it.
> No longer longing for what could have been.
> The greater blessing is in our future not our past.
> The greater blessing is in fruitfulness.

Day 7

STRENGTH   For Joseph to fulfill his destiny, he had to forgive, forget, and bear new fruit.
What is God showing you to forgive and forget?
What new fruit will you believe for?

STAND   FORGIVING

STAND   FORGETFUL

STAND   FRUITFUL

DAY 8

HOLD TIGHT

Hebrews 5:12

"living and powerful and sharper than any two-edged sword."

Many valiant men fought in God's army under King David. The Lord's army was large and loyal at that time. Among them all were three mighty men God used to defeat the enemy in dramatic ways.

One of these three was Eleazar. He inspires me. He was with David when the Philistines were defeated. All of the other men of Israel had retreated, but Eleazar *"arose and attacked the Philistines until his hand was weary and his hand stuck to the sword."* Through Eleazar's faithfulness, *"The Lord brought about a great victory that day"* (2 Samuel 23:10).

> You and I are also called to enlist in the army of the Lord.
> According to our Commander-in-Chief, the weapons of our warfare are not carnal, but mighty.
> Ephesians 6:17 instructs us to take up a sword as Eleazar did, however, our sword
> *"is the sword of the spirit, which is the Word of God."*

Open the palm of your hand and think what it would be like to hold a sword so long and so tightly that it became imbedded into your hand. That sword is now a part of you.

Day 8

A memory comes of when my daughter was little and she would want me to hold her and carry her constantly. There would be times that my arm would become fixed in the position I held her. I would lose feeling in my arm and it would remain in that fixed position long after I had sat her down.

You get it.
God wants us to so faithfully and lovingly uphold the
Word of God that it becomes fixed in us!

He says, *"receive with meekness the implanted word which is able to save your souls."* James 1:2

Far too often we try to fight the enemy with our own weapons of human effort, only to be defeated again and again. Christ faced the enemy in the wilderness and He was victorious with the very weapon He tells us to take hold of.

Christ overcame the enemy with the Word of God.
Christ said over and over,
"It is written . . ." (Matthew 4:1–11).

Like Eleazar, you are heroic when you hold fast to the
Word of the Lord until the victory is complete.
Your Sword is powerful. Your part is to hold on!

The Word is . . . *"living and powerful and sharper than any two-edged sword."* Hebrews 5:12

Day 8

STRENGTH   God's Word is Almighty!

STAND   Hold fast to the Word of the Lord for each battle, each day.

STAND   Victoriously upholding His Word!

Day 9

SAME POWER

Ephesians 1:19–20

"I also pray that you will understand the incredible greatness of God's power for us who believe him. This is the same mighty power that raised Christ from the dead and seated him in the place of honor at God's right hand . . ."

As we accept the truth that we will be persecuted for righteousness sake we realize that we have no idea how to handle whatever our persecution may look like. Yet this encouraging scripture directs our hearts to know that we are not alone.

Christian song writer, Jeremy Camp, was performing amid opposition in a foreign country and he testifies that he was able to press through knowing that the same power that raised Christ from the dead lived in him.

> The verses of his song inspire and encourage us to take hold of this truth and **STAND**.

Day 9

SAME POWER
Jeremy Camp

"I can see – Waters raging at my feet
I can feel – The breath of those surrounding me
I can hear – The sounds of nations rising up.
We will not be overtaken
We will not be overcome
If I can walk – Down this dark and narrow road
I can face – Every fear of the unknown
I can hear – All God's children singing out
We will not be overtaken
We will not be overcome

The same power that rose Jesus from the grave
The same power that commands the dead to wake
Lives in us, lives in us
The same power that moves mountains when He speaks
Lives in us, lives in us
He lives in us, lives in us

We have hope – That His promises are true
In His strength – There is nothing we can't do
Yes we know – There are greater things in store
We will not be overtaken
We will not be overcome
Greater is He that is living in me
He conquered our enemy
No power of darkness – No weapon prevails
We stand here in victory!"

Day 9

STRENGTH   We can **Stand** because
Greater is He that is living in us!
Christ in us is the answer.
We can **Stand** because Christ is victorious over all things—past, present, and future!

STAND   No matter the opposition!

STAND   In the same mighty power that rose Jesus from the grave!

(Thank you, Jeremy Camp,
for your encouraging song, "Same Power".)

Day 10

AS ONE

John 17:21

"that they all may be one as You, Father are in Me, and I in You; that they also may be one in Us, that the world may believe that You sent Me."

Christ is a great intercessor.
He prayed and Lazarus walked out of the tomb.
He prayed and Peter turned from coward to courage.
He prayed and men were delivered of demons.
He prayed and we are becoming ONE!

I have witnessed this miracle. A Jewish man who became a Believer in Christ (Messianic Jew) with his arms around a former Muslim who also is now a Believer in Christ (Muslim Background Believer, MBB) with over 3000 Gentile Believers in Christ from 170 nations.

ALL
taking communion together!
Jew, Arab, and Gentile,
All celebrating the love of Christ!

I will never be the same!
We are ONE!

Day 10

As the world gets darker the light of Christ shines brighter. Seeing people who should be enemies laugh and rejoice together is joyous! The Word of God encourages us that the JOY of the Lord is our
STRENGTH
(Nehemiah 8:10).

We have **STRENGTH** when we have God's joy and His joy comes when we see His love displayed in the lives of His people.
God tells us that LOVE never fails
(I Corinthians 13:8).

When we see the love of Christ making enemies friends we have
STRENGTH to STAND.

Do you have an enemy?
Are you open to a miracle?
Pray and give Christ permission to make your enemy your friend.

Be willing to have your heart changed by God's love.
He will give you His eyes to see your enemy the way He sees them.
Love does not fail!

Day 10

STRENGTH   Christ has prayed and ONENESS is now real.

STAND   AS ONE with others in Christ

STAND   Let His Love and Joy bring ONENESS through your life.

STAND   Christ is glorified when we are AS ONE!

(Thank you Aglow International for this genuine
AS ONE experience!)
Aglow International Conference 2015

Day 11

LIKE ISRAEL

Genesis 12: 3

*"I will bless those who bless you,
And I will curse him who curses you,
And in you all the families of the earth
shall be blessed."*

A few years ago I realized that I am as old as Israel!

I was born in 1948 and Israel was recognized again as a nation in 1948. I have also begun to research my ancestry because my father is German and I believe that I may be a German Jew.

It is amusing to think I am as old as this ancient nation and then sobering as I think of all that Israel has overcome and become in the years we have shared. Daily Israel must **STAND** and fight just to exist. I have been blessed to visit the land of Israel three times and each time felt "I was home."

> God promises to "bless" those who bless Israel. To "bless" Israel is to **STAND** with Israel.

Day 11

God calls us to support this chosen nation in every way possible. **STAND** praying for them as they are threatened daily by the surrounding nations who purpose to destroy them. **STAND** believing in God's faithfulness to sustain them and fulfill His promises to them and for them. **STAND** praying for the people of the Land to know their Messiah, Christ Jesus.

The name ISRAEL means *"who prevails with God."*
We each are Israeli when we choose
to **STAND** and prevail with God for His chosen people,
ISRAEL.
We are to **STAND** by them, for them, and with them.

According to God's Word, every person who has received Christ as their Savior has been *"grafted in"* to His promises and destiny for Israel, (Romans 11).

We each have a personal stake in **STANDING** with God's chosen people. When we do, we are partakers in their blessings.

Day 11

STRENGTH It is a privilege to prevail with God for His people ISRAEL.
We are "grafted in" by His grace.
Receive the blessings as you fulfill God's Word.
Recognize your privileged position

STAND Fulfill your calling to ISRAEL

STAND Prevail in Prayer for ISRAEL

Day 12

LOVED

Romans 8:38–39

"For I am sure that neither death nor life, nor angels nor rulers, nor things present nor things to come, nor powers, nor height nor depth, nor anything else in all creation, will be able to separate us from the love of God in Christ Jesus our Lord."

I have the humble privilege of personally knowing a courageous woman who converted from Islam to Christianity. She was raised in a Muslim family, lived in a Muslim nation, was married to a Muslim man, and was even a teacher of Islam herself. She seemed destined to live out her life as a follower of Mohammad. However, God who *"foreknew her and predestined her"* knew exactly when and how to bring her to salvation in Christ.

She shares that living in Islam she never knew love and was never told she was loved. Then God chose the perfect day and time to reveal His love to her. As with many Muslims, God appeared supernaturally to her and embraced her in His love. Today she herself radiates God's love and the light of His Word.

God truly is Almighty.
God knew my friend and knew exactly how and when
To make Himself known to her through His love.

Day 12

Today this former Muslim is fully confident of God's love for her and this confidence has enabled her to withstand horrific persecution. She repeatedly has been raped, beaten, and poisoned and as a mother has had to endure seeing her children beaten for their faith as well. Yet, this courageous devoted disciple of Christ **stands** in the power of God's love declaring,

*"There IS a price to pay, but we have eternal life!
I am Silent No More!"*

God assures us in 1Corinthians 13:8, *"That love never fails."*

His love has never failed my friend.
She is able now to faithfully **STAND** in her love for Him.
Her enduring love has become an inspiration for many throughout the world.
Myself included!
She is a living testimony of God's love and faithfulness.

Day 12

STRENGTH   *"Love endures all things."* 1Corinthians 13:4

STAND   Confident in His love.

STAND   Faithful in return.

(Thank you, "my friend" for standing
so courageously & faithfully. You truly are inspiring!
Name withheld to protect identity.)

Day 13

ESSENCE

Revelation 19:7

*". . . for the marriage of the Lamb has come,
and His bride has made herself ready."*

Study the scripture above, it does not say "wedding" but "marriage."
It is crucial that we distinguish between the two.
A wedding is a onetime shared special event.
A marriage is a lifetime relationship.
Do you see the difference?

The definition of the word "essence" is "that which makes a thing what it is."
The Lord has given me an awareness of my essence.
Actually, we all share this essence.
Our essence is that we are the chosen bride of Christ.

A bride is to live out of the essence of being chosen, beloved and sought out (Isaiah 62).
Her delight is to be in her bridegroom not the wedding.
The bride has a single focus, preparation for life with her Bridegroom.
We see this portrayed very well in the story of Esther.
She prepared for a full year and her only concern was
"if it pleases the King"
(Esther 5:4).

Day 13

Many brides and grooms are too busy preparing for the one day wedding event and not preparing themselves for a lifetime relationship with one another. The wedding event does not make the marriage.

In the church the same thing seems to happen. We come to Christ through a salvation (love) experience and have a brief time of excitement over being "born again", chosen by Him. Then we get busy doing things. Good things. We go to Bible study, teach Sunday school, usher, join the worship team, offer help, pray for the sick, etc. But in all of this busyness, we often lose our focus and end up with our personal relationship to our Bridegroom becoming lifeless and loveless.

> Our marriage is not to the church but to the
> Bridegroom of the church.
> Our essence is found in being His
> not in what we are doing in His family.

> Christ wants our hearts occupied with knowing Him.
> Our worship is to be one dimensional for He is our One-an-Only.
> Our good works are then an out flow of our
> RELATIONSHIP with Him.
> Our heart is to remain fixed on Him.
> Our identity, *essence*, is in being His.

Day 13

STRENGTH In His letter to the church of Ephesus, Christ says *". . . I have this one charge to make against you, that you have left (abandoned) the love you had at first for me, your first love . . . return to Me . . ."* Revelation 2:4–5 Amp.

STAND Embrace your *essence* continually.

STAND Married to Him.

Day 14

MOST BLESSED

Judges 5:24

"most blessed among women is Jael..."

What about this woman would cause the Word of God to so praise her?

Judges 5:24–27 reveals how courageous she was when the enemy of God came into her life...

*"She stretched her hand to the tent peg,
her right hand to the workman's hammer.
She pounded Sisera, she pierced his head,
she split and struck through his temple.
At her feet he sank, he lay still; at her feet he sank, he fell;
where he sank there he fell dead."*

What motivated this woman to such extreme action? Often during this period of history, names were a reflection of the character of the person. This is true of Jael.

Her name means *"beneficial"*.

And God praised her because the whole nation of Israel benefitted from her bravery.
When the enemy of the Kingdom of God came to her dwelling place, she rose up and took the Kingdom by violence.

Day 14

"And from the days of John the Baptist until now the kingdom of heaven suffers violence, and the violent take it by force"
(Matthew 11:12).

Yes, God reveals that throughout time the Kingdom of God will suffer violence and we are called to be the violent who take it by force. Truly, there are times and places in our current world that you may have to be as Jael and use physical violence to defend your life and the Kingdom. Each of us must defend the Kingdom of God daily. The battle is ever present! We must be battle-minded and prepared to take our **STAND**.

Meditations, thoughts, ideas will often come to our mind
which are enemies of the Kingdom of God within us.
Just as Siseria sought refuge in Jael's home,
Satan seeks to invade the privacy and security of our minds.

When these enemies come, God is looking for us to be as Jael.
Be *"beneficial"* to the Kingdom of God.
Use the weapons of our warfare.
Pull down these strongholds.
Take every enemy thought captive.

Jael used a tent peg and hammer to overcome the enemy.
The weapons of our warfare are not carnal, but mighty.
We have the Word of God.
That we use through the power of the Holy Spirit.

Day 14

STRENGTH *"For the weapons of our warfare are not carnal but mighty in God for pulling down strongholds, casting down arguments and every high and lofty thing that exalts itself against the knowledge of God, bringing every thought into captivity to the obedience of Christ."*
2 Corinthians 10:4–5

STAND Resist the enemy of your heart, mind, and life with the Word of God.

STAND Be ***"beneficial"*** for the Kingdom of God.

STAND Be " most blessed"!

DAY 15

DENY SELF

Luke 9:23
*"Deny yourself take up your cross daily,
and follow me."*

Keith Green was a 90's Christian musician who along with blessing the Kingdom of God with some incredible music made a strong statement of faith that is a call and a challenge to all of us.

When Keith gave his life to Jesus he also laid down his music.
He was willing to never pick it up again.
God showed him that it could be his idol.
It caused people to idolize him and his music rather than Christ.
Keith wanted to lead others to Christ not to music or himself.
Keith wanted NO idolatry in his life.

Eventually God released him to perform his music again and he immediately "made it big" in Christian music. But when others would ask him how to succeed in music he would ask them a series of probing questions:
Are you willing to never play music again?
Are you willing to be nothing?
Are you willing to go *anywhere* and do *anything* for Christ?
Are you willing to stay right where you are
let the Lord do great things through you
even though no one may seem to notice at all?

Day 15

Keith's defining statement was, "I repent of ever having recorded one single song, and ever having performed one concert, if my music, and most importantly, my life have not provoked you to sell out more completely to Jesus."

He said, *"When I die I want to be remembered as a Christian.*

"Let me say that the only music minister to whom the Lord will say,
'Well done, thy good and faithful servant',
is the one whose life proves what their lyrics are saying, and the one to whom music is the least important part of their life."

"Glorifying the only worthy One has to be the most important goal.
Let us not forget that our due service to the Lord is not only to live for Him
'but also to suffer for His sake'"
(Philippians 1:29).

Keith then concludes with this compelling call . . . *"Let us die graciously together and endure to the end like brave soldiers who give their lives, without hesitation, for our noble and glorious King of Light."*

Day 15

STRENGTH   How do you want to be remembered?
             What idols need to come down?

STAND   Willing to *"suffer for His sake"*.

STAND   Deny self, take up your cross, follow Him.

Day 16

P-U-S-H

Isaiah 62:1, 6–7

*"For Zion's sake I will not keep silent, and for Jerusalem's sake I will not keep quiet, **until** her righteousness goes forth like brightness ... On her walls, Oh Jerusalem, I have appointed watchmen, all **day and all night** they will never keep silent. You who remind the Lord, **take no rest for yourselves**; And give Him no rest until He establishes and makes Jerusalem a praise in the earth."*

To pray **day and night** means to pray UNTIL.
Until you know that the will of God has been fulfilled.
Until you know God has released you from the intercession.
Until you know the Spirit of God has moved.

Christ did not say, "if you pray" but **when you pray**. To Christ it was just a given that His disciples would pray. Jesus instructed the disciples ... Matthew 6:

"when you pray" (vs 5)
"when you pray" (vs 6)
"when you pray" (vs 7)
And the disciples got it! In Acts 6:4 they said
"we give ourselves **continually** to prayer ..."

Day 16

I like this analogy . . .

P-U-S-H – PRAY **U**NTIL **S**OMETHING **H**APPENS

God makes a powerful promise of response to faithful
PUSHING PRAYER

"If my people who are called by my name, will humble themselves and pray and seek my face and turn from their wicked ways, then I will hear from heaven and I will forgive their sin and heal their land."
2 Chronicles 7:14

When we PRAY we Take A **STAND** before God saying that
we **know** He cares,
He has the power,
and that He alone is the answer.
We reveal our Faith In Him
When we Pray UNTIL.

Day 16

STRENGTH   Our prayer life reveals our relationship with God through Time, Faith, and Trust

STAND   Reveal your Trust as you **Pray** continually.

STAND   Strengthen your Faith as you **Pray** day and night

STAND   Enjoy your personal Time with Him as you **Pray** UNTIL

Day 17

PRESSED

Luke 22:42–44 Amp.

"Father, if You are willing, remove this cup from Me; yet not My will, but [always] Yours be done. And there appeared to Him an angel from heaven, strengthening Him in Spirit. And being in an agony [of mind], He prayed [all the] more earnestly and intently, and His sweat became like great clots of blood dropping down upon the ground."

Here in the Garden called Gethsemane, Jesus wrestled with the battle of His will and God's will. The part of Christ that was "fully man" feared He could not live up to the expectations that the Father had for the "fully God" part of Him.

I am so grateful for this honest, real, true, human part of Christ. The truth is I do not always trust that I can be as strong or faithful as God wants me to be. In Gethsemane, Jesus knew what God wanted but He also knew that He could be real with the Father about his fears, weaknesses, and doubts.

The word "Gethsemane" means "the oil **press**." In this garden the olives would be removed from the trees and then **"pressed"** until the necessary oil came forth.

Day 17

Christ was **pressed** in Gethsemane as well. The battle between the flesh and the Spirit was intense and even though God had compassion and sent an angel to comfort His Son, the **pressing** continued until the oil of obedience flowed.

The truth is that when we pray we often are subconsciously expecting God to do things our way.
Give us what we want. Make us happy.
We pray expecting God to perform our will on earth.
We each will be **pressed** by the Spirit for the obedience that God needs from us for the battles of life He has called us to.
These life and death battles are ones we would prefer to avoid, just as Christ honestly revealed in the Garden.

It is God's will that the Kingdom of God come on earth through our obedience just as it did through Christ.

As we see the reality of Christ in Gethsemane we see that God will not remove the challenge but will comfort us in it and enable us to **"press"** through into obedience.
Through obedience comes the Victory!

Day 17

STRENGTH   Christ understands your fears.
Stand
You can be real with God.
Stand

In the **pressing** times . . . **STAND.**

Day 18

SCARY AS HELL

2 Timothy 1:7

"For God has not given us a spirit of fear, but of power, and of love and of a sound mind."

The world is scary as hell. Love anyway.
By Jeremy Courtney
November 17, 2015
The Washington Post

"If you're not afraid, you're either braver than me or significantly less informed."

This is the confession in the article above. I was impressed and relieved to find this honesty in this report.

Jeremy Courtney who writes this article goes on to say that he lives with his family in Iraq, working at the headwaters of the Syrian and Iraqi refugee crisis, moving among Sunni jihadist sniper fire, suicide bombers, sleeper cells and Iranian-backed militia. He has received death threats, had mobs incited against him, and had friends kidnapped and killed. And he admits he is afraid. Yet, he is there. He loves anyway.

Day 18

He goes on in his article to say, "Terrorism is terrifying. But we should aim to not be ruled by fear. In the face of ISIS, Iran and countless other nemesis neighbors, we commit to love anyway."

The World is scary as hell!

I love the truth in his statements. He is afraid but he is not ruled by fear. God does not want us to pretend and deny reality. We are to admit feelings of fear but not give into a "spirit of fear" which paralyzes us.

> God gives us His **power,**
> His ability to **love,**
> and His **sound mind**

Day 18

STRENGTH With His POWER we have the
Strength to Stand

With His LOVE we have the
Strength to Stand

With His SOUND MIND we have the
Strength to Stand

STAND You do not have a spirit of fear.

STAND In His POWER through His LOVE with His WISDOM.

Day 19

KING OF GLORY

Psalm 24:10

"Who is this King of Glory?
The Lord of Hosts, He is the King of Glory."

Yahweh tasaba'ot is Hebrew for "Lord of Hosts. It reveals that God rules over all armies. The armies of Heaven (Revelation 19:14), the armies of Israel (Joshua 5:14), the hosts of the nations (Jeremiah 3:19), and of everything in heaven and earth (Genesis 2:1) all are subject to the Captain, Christ Jesus (Hebrew2:10).

Christ has lead captivity captive (Ephesians 4:8).

Made a show of the enemy openly triumphing over him in it (Colossians 2:15).

He has taken the keys of authority and given them to His church (Matthew 16:19)

Who is this King of Glory?
He is the triumphant Jesus who has purchased your salvation and has given you access to the very throne of God.
(Hebrews 4:16)

Day 19

Psalm 24 calls to you: *"Lift up your heads, O you gates!*
And be lifted up, you everlasting doors!
And the King of glory shall come in!"

Christ, your King, desires to come into your life and triumph gloriously over sin, sickness, darkness and despair. He will come bringing His Kingdom of righteousness, peace and joy.

Open your heart, Open you mind, Open fully to
His Lordship of Love.

"The Lord strong and mighty, The Lord mighty in battle"
Psalm 24:8.

Is there an area of your life not yet open to the King of Glory?

The Lord of Hosts reigns in His love.

Open to the triumph of His love in EVERY area of your life!

Day 19

STRENGTH   Let the kingdoms of your world become the kingdoms of your Lord and Christ.
Let the King of Glory reign fully in your life.
Revelation 11:15

STAND   It is time.

STAND   Open yourself fully to this One who is greater than all that comes against you.

STAND   May the King of Glory rule and reign!

Day 20

LOOK UP

Luke 21:28

"Now when these things begin to happen, look up and lift up your heads, because your redemption draws near."

With these words Christ was giving direction to His disciples about things to come that still apply to us today.

LOOK UP!

There are many things happening in our world that can tempt us to look down, be depressed, and feel discouraged.

But our Lord says, LOOK UP!

"Lift up your heads, oh you gates!
And be lifted up, you everlasting doors!
And the King of glory shall come in.
Who is this King of glory!
The Lord strong and mighty,
The Lord mighty in battle.
Lift up your heads, O you gates!
Lift up, you everlasting doors!
And the King of glory shall come in.
Who is this King of glory?
The Lord of hosts,
He is the King of glory."
Psalm 24:7–9

Day 20

We, the Believers, are the gates.
God wants to reveal Himself to the world through our hearts.

It is essential that we lift up our spirits in time of trouble and reveal our faith and hope in Him.

Those who do not know the Lord are hopeless.
We carry Hope in times of darkness.

We lift our heads and encourage others because we know
Christ triumphs gloriously.
We lift our heads and His love and hope are reflected to those
who are lost.
We lift our heads and reveal mercy and goodness
in times of distress.
We open our lives for Him to live through and the lost come into
His Kingdom!

DAY 20

STRENGTH See your purpose.
You are a gate of His glory.
Open wide – Live boldly for Christ!
Let His love and light shine.
LOOK UP with hope and faith.

STAND Big, Bold and Believing!

STAND LOOK UP – HE IS COMING!

Day 21

BADGE OF HONOR

2 Timothy 3:12

"In fact, everyone who wants to live a godly life in Christ Jesus will be persecuted . . ."

"No more prayers or else . . ."

Yes, this is the notice that a High School Football Coach received in the state of Washington in the fall of 2015. The coach simply would kneel and pray at the end of the game. Sometimes players from both teams would willing join him. Now, he has received notice that he cannot kneel and pray or he risks being fired.

What would you do? Think about it.

Your job, income, livelihood is on the line.

Will you kneel and pray? Will you publically live your out your faith?

How sad but real that the United States of America now threatens a believer in Christ who publically takes a **STAND** for his faith. Our constitution says that we have "freedom of religion". Yet, now, when that freedom is acted on we may actually be persecuted.

The truth is that our world has changed and the freedoms that our constitution guaranteed are now conditional. None of this takes our God by surprise. The Word tells us that our Lord sees the end from the beginning. The founders of this nation hoped that there truly could

Day 21

be a nation where there was freedom to worship, but God reveals in His Word that all will be tested and persecuted. Therefore, God knew that our freedoms would be temporary.

I confess, it has been nice to grow-up in a country where I had religious freedom.

I could openly worship my God both privately and publically.

But that country no longer exists.

America has changed.

I now know that I will be persecuted right here in the good old USA for my faith in Christ.

A page of history has turned and the Kingdom battle is now being openly waged in my

No-longer free nation.

God warned us of "such a time as this." He tells us throughout His Word that we, the believers in Christ, will suffer persecution. We should not be surprised. But most of us have had it so easy for so long that we truly did not expect to be raped of our freedom in our life time.

Persecution is an honor.
It is an honor to have enough evidence in your life to be found guilty of living your life for Christ!

Day 21

STRENGTH   I now recognize persecution as a "badge of honor." Congratulations to the Coach!
Thanks for **STANDING!**

STAND   Guilty as charged for living for Christ!

STAND   Receive your "badge of honor".

DAY 22

COVER AND CARRY

Numbers 4:4

"This is the service . . . in the tabernacle of meeting relating to the most holy things."

Most of us have heard the saying, "change is inevitable" or "you can count on things changing." Change truly is constant in all areas of life.

As real as change is, many of us are resistant to change. Change can strain relationships, bring disunity, insecurity and fear. This is true within our own selves, our family, church, job, or friendships. Yet, because change is a reality of life we must prepare to do it as well as possible.

Here in Numbers 4 we find God revealing a huge routine of change. The Israelites were on their journey to the Promised Land, a huge change in the pattern of their lives. God would lead them with a cloud by day and a pillar of fire by night. There were three families of Levites, whose sole duty was to *"cover and carry"* the holy things for the move of God. They were responsible to prepare, protect, and transport the tabernacle of God for each step of the change.

The priests who *"covered and carried"* the holy things numbered 22,000 men between the ages of 30 and 50. They were mature and strong.

It is a mark of maturity when you can handle change well.

Day 22

> You are the *"temple of the living God"* (I Corinthians 3:16).
> You are *"a holy priesthood"* (1Peter 2:9).
> God is taking you from "glory to glory" (2 Corinthians 3:18).
> So what within you needs *"covered and carried"*
> when change takes place?
> What is it in you that God considers "the holy things"?

During change we must protect, prepare and transport our heart attitude, our emotions, and our thinking. It is the inner man of our heart and mind that must be covered in prayer and carefully carried in righteousness by the Spirit so that we arrive whole and holy.

The weight of the holy things was enormous, well over 10 tons. We must be strong in the power of His might to bear the weight of preserving unity, righteousness, and faith as we endure the inevitable changes of life.

God is aware that change is difficult and He guarantees He will provide what we need by His Holy Spirit, just as He did for the Levites. He will lead and guide us and strengthen us for the move. He will give us great wisdom in *"covering and carrying"* those things that are holy in His sight. His desire is that our hearts be the tabernacle of His presence and that we be prepared to move with Him as He moves in our world.

Day 22

STRENGTH   What is changing in your world?
Do you need to adjust the way you
"cover and carry" at this time?

STAND   Trust God to lead and guide you.

STAND   Guard your heart and mind
"Trust in the Lord with all of your heart"
(Proverbs 3:5).

Day 23

HARD HEARTS

Mark 3:5 NKJV

". . . being grieved by the hardness of their hearts . . ."

I know a mother with two children who was forced to live in a homeless shelter for three years. She was forced by hard hearts. Her husband had abandoned her and their children for a relationship with another man. Then when she divorced him, her church-going, Bible-believing mother refused to let her own daughter and grand children live with her because she didn't believe in divorce.

The Gospels reveal Christ was **angry** at the "religious" people who objected to Him and his disciples picking grain to eat on the Sabbath and of Him healing a man on the Sabbath. Christ revealed that legalistic, religious thinking had hardened their hearts.

In I Corinthians 13, the Apostle Paul says, *". . . though I speak with tongues of men and of angels, but have not love, I have become sounding brass or a clanging cymbal . . . without love, it profits me nothing."*

God grieves when we persecute one another because of religion. Even though persecution is never pleasant, we somewhat expect those of other beliefs to persecute us. But persecution from within the Body of Christ is persecution that never should happen. Sadly, I have seen too many examples. And I know hard hearts never please God.

Day 23

As Christians we are to love one another and even bless our enemies. Christ is glorified not when we are legalistic but when the Church sets the bar to love like no one else in the world knows how to love.

People will want to become part of the "family of God" when the "family of God" is the safest place on earth.

The woman in this story has grown in God and forgiven her mother. Her heart has not hardened because she has important memories of her father who died long before all of this happened.

When times were difficult in the homeless shelter she would cuddle under a down comforter where she would remember her father and his love. Her natural father was not legalistic but loving.

Because her natural father's heart was not hard she can now receive the comfort and healing of Father God's love.

Day 23

STRENGTH Cuddle in the truth of God's love.
Lay down judgment and legalism.
Do not let your heart be hardened.

STAND With a heart of compassion.

STAND Let God love through you.

Day 24

ROCK FORMATION

Matthew 16:18–19

"And I tell you that you are Peter, and on this rock I will build my church, and the gates of Hades will not overcome it."

This is an encouraging and hopeful story. The disciple that Christ called a ***rock*** was really just an ordinary guy who was willing to be changed by Christ. Does that sound like you?

When Christ first met Peter his name was Simon. The meaning of the name Simon was "the name of nine". It meant that he was just an ordinary guy. But once this ordinary guy met Jesus his life began to change and he eventually became who Christ said he was, the ***Rock***.

When I think of this, I think,
"Me Too!"

I want to become who Christ says I am.

Impulsive Peter went from cutting off a man's ear in anger to three times denying he even knew Christ to being the one who healed others, lead many to salvation and then chose to die upside down on a cross because he was not worthy to die in the same position as Christ.

Simon truly became a **Rock** for others to **Stand** upon.

How did this all happen?

Day 24

In Luke, we find Christ encouraging Peter that He has been praying for him and reassuring him that he would make it.

"Simon, Simon! Indeed Satan has asked for you, that he may sift you as wheat. But I have prayed for you, that your faith should not fail; and when you have returned to Me, strengthen your brethren."
Luke 22:31–32

In Hebrews Christ reassures us that He is also faithfully interceding for you and me.

"Therefore He is also able to save to the uttermost those who come to God through Him, since He always lives to make intercession for them."
Hebrews 7:25

We, too, can **STAND** because the One who is **strong** is ever interceding for us.

By the Spirit, He lives within us, prays for us, and is fully faithful to us.

Like Peter, through the faithful intercession of Christ, we have

Strength to Stand.

After Christ prayed for Peter he then instructed Peter to

"Strengthen his brothers."

Day 24

STRENGTH	As we each receive God's **Strength** to **STAND** we are to **strengthen** our brothers as well.
STAND	Encourage one another, build one another up in the faith . . . be a **ROCK!**
STAND	Pray one for another.

Day 25

JUST SUPPOSE

Matthew 24:9

"Then they will hand you over to be persecuted . . ."

Just suppose persecution comes to your door step. Just suppose that our nation is overtaken by an enemy of our God. Just suppose that your church was put on lock-down. Just suppose you are taken by authorities and interrogated because you wear a cross around your neck and have a faith-based bumper sticker on your car.

The truth is that neither you nor I want to think about these possibilities. We do not know what sacrifice is. We do not really experience suffering. We have not yet been persecuted for our beliefs. We have been free and blessed.

The Reverend Billy Graham says, "The immunity to persecution that Christians in America have experienced in the past two centuries is unusual. Christ strongly warned all Christians that to follow Him would not be popular and that in most circumstances it would mean cross-bearing and persecution."

Graham goes on to say, "Since we have experienced little religious persecution in this country, it is likely that under pressure many would deny Christ. Those who shout the loudest about their faith may surrender the soonest. Many who boast of being courageous would be cowardly." (BGM Mainsite, Prepare+For+Persecution)

Day 25

We have no Biblical foundation for thinking we can escape being persecuted for our faith in Christ. The **normal** for Christians from the time of Christ until now is persecution.

The big question is not **if** but **when** and **how.**

Recently a friend at church made a thought provoking statement, "Many say they want to live for Christ, but I have never heard anyone say they are willing to die for Him."

As I process all of this, I think part of the answer is that we are called by God to die daily.

We are to die to self and live for Christ each and every day. God's ways are not our ways, they are far above our ways (Isaiah 5:9) and we are to be living for Him and revealing Him through the way we live, treat others, and make choices, each and every day.

> I believe that as we daily die to self and live for Christ it will prepare us for the persecution that comes.

Day 25

STRENGTH — *"For I am persuaded that neither death nor life, nor angels, nor principalities nor powers, nor things present nor things to come, nor height nor depth, nor any other created thing, shall be able to separate us from the love of God which is in Christ Jesus our Lord"* Romans 8:38–39.

STAND — Daily . . . Living for Christ . . .

Day 26

DECIDED

Colossians 3:2
"Set your mind on things above."

Assam lived in the nation of India where head-hunting was a part of the culture. When he and his family converted to Christianity, the village chief commanded him to renounce Christ or be beheaded.

Assam's response was,
"I have decided to follow Jesus."

When his wife was killed, he said
"Though none go with me, still I will follow."

Then, as Assam, himself, was executed, he sang,
"The cross before me, the world behind me."

Assam's courageous display of faith resulted in the village chief and others in the village converting to Christ. As Assam's testimony was shared, his declarations were made into a song that has been sung throughout the Body of Christ for years.

Day 26

Sing with me . . .

I HAVE DECIDED TO FOLLOW JESUS

I have decided to follow Jesus;
I have decided to follow Jesus;
I have decided to follow Jesus;
No turning back, no turning back.

Though I may wonder, I still will follow;
Though I may wonder, I still will follow;
Though I may wonder, I still will follow;
No turning back, no turning back.

The world behind me, the cross before me;
The world behind me, the cross before me;
The world behind me, the cross before me;
No turning back, no turning back.

Though none go with me, still I will follow;
Though none go with me, still I will follow;
Though none go with me, still I will follow;
No turning back, no turning back.

Will you decide now to follow Jesus?
Will you decide now to follow Jesus?
Will you decide now to follow Jesus?
No turning back, no turning back.

Day 26

STRENGTH Set your mind.
Make the DECISION.
Feel the **Strength**.

STAND No Turning Back

STAND No Turning Back

Day 27

KINGDOM AGAINST KINGDOM

Matthew 24:7
*"Nation will rise against nation,
and kingdom against kingdom."*

Most everyone can remember where they were on 9/11.
I was in my home, for some reason not working that day.
My husband called and anxiously said, "Turn on the TV!"
I watched the TV, talked to my best friend,
no one knew what to think.
I drove to my church, laid on my face,
asking God what was happening.
What did this mean?
Then, oh so gently, the Lord spoke,
"Kingdom against Kingdom."
I understood.

I understood because I had become very informed about Islam.

I understood that Islam is an anti-Christ religion.

So I knew that God was revealing that the

Kingdom of the Anti-Christ was attacking the Kingdom of God.

I realized that a dramatic shift had taken place in our world and things would never be the same. We were one step closer to what the Bible reveals in Matthew 24 as the *End of the Age*.

Day 27

Matthew 24 reveals the progression of the end,
"wars and rumors of wars."
Yes, I was born just after WWII, knew of the Korean War, graduated college during the Vietnam War and was living with the effects of the Gulf War.
Nation had indeed been against nation.

But on 9/11

It was now... "Kingdom against Kingdom".
A progressive step to end times.

"Then you will be handed over to be persecuted and put to death, and you will be hated by all nations because of me."
Matthew 24:9

Here we are, today within in our own nation, today the Kingdom battle rages. Our nation that was founded on Christian freedom and known as *"one nation under God"* now persecutes Christian business owners for upholding their Biblical beliefs, uses Sharia (Islamic) law in its courts, forbids Christian prayer in our public schools and restrains the use of the Bible in the military.

Christ continues to explain it all in Matthew 24:10–12 *". . . many will turn away from the faith and will betray and hate each other . . . because of the increase of wickedness, the love of most will grow cold."*

Day 27

STRENGTH God prepares us and encourages us.
"*See, I have told you ahead of time*" Matthew 24:25.

STAND "*but he who **stands** firm to the end will be saved. And the gospel of the kingdom will be preached in the whole world as a testimony to all nations, and then the end will come*" Matthew 24:13–14.

STAND Faithful because Christ is preparing us.

Day 28

DESTINY

2 Corinthians 12:9

". . . My grace is sufficient for you, for my strength is made perfect in weakness."

Thankfully, I have not yet experienced actual war. Probably most reading this devotional have not as well. But I have a dear friend who knows what it is to have God's grace to **STAND** in a time of actual war.

As my friend describes her time in Israel during the 2006 Israeli summer war with Hezbollah fighters in Lebanon she says, *"There is no safer place to be than in the center of God's will."*

This war was part of her DESTINY.

While serving with a Ministry in Israel she, her husband and 11 year old daughter took in Lebanese refugees, Russian Jews, Arabs and others during the bombings in the city of Haifa in northern Israel. Their Ministry provided food, clothing, shelter, diapers, toys and comfort for those caught in the war. Daily they would hear the sirens and hustle those in their care to the bomb shelter and continue to provide for them there. The Israeli Jets flew over day and night taking out enemy rocket launchers. Yet, the most difficult part was the stifling heat and lack of air in the bomb shelter.

Day 28

My friend describes that "the grace of God took over and we were able to take care of others and not be afraid. We were able to *dig-in with them* rather than leave and we were respected for that and were a witness of God's love."

His grace is sufficient for the DESTINY He calls us to.

When the bombings began my friend and her family were at a movie theater. The movie was interrupted with an announcement about the bombings. They went outside the theater amid the confusion and felt the fear of what was happening but immediately the grace of God came upon them and the fear left.

My courageous friend quotes this Psalm as a testimony . . .

Psalm 27:1,   *"The Lord is my light and my salvation;*
              Whom shall I fear?
              The Lord is the strength of my life,
              Of whom shall I be afraid?"

Day 28

STRENGTH We do not know what wars we will face.
But you can be assured that He has prepared the
GRACE necessary for your DESTINY.

STAND by His GRACE

STAND in your DESTINY

(Thank you, my inspiring friend,
for standing in your Destiny.
God and I both know who you are!)

Day 29

I KNOW

2 Timothy 1: 12

"For this reason I also suffer these things; nevertheless I am not ashamed, for I know whom I have believed and am persuaded that He is able to keep what I have committed to Him until that Day."

The scripture above is part of a letter that the Apostle Paul wrote to his friend Timothy to encourage and instruct him on how to **STAND** during uncertain times. Paul was in prison at the time he wrote this letter. The one in prison is encouraging the one who does not know what is to come. We can identify. At this time, many are being persecuted and even imprisoned for their faith, and we do not know what to expect.

I saw this reminder of our world circumstances the other day and it truly made me pause and think:

USA
9/11

FRANCE
11/15

ISRAEL
24/7

Day 29

Paul's encouragement to Timothy was based on *"I know whom I have believed . . ."*

Paul had the **STRENGTH to STAND** because he truly knew the one he was **STANDING** for. This is also our answer as well.

The more fully we know our God, His heart and purposes, the more fully we will be *"persuaded"* to believe in Him and to **STAND** as faithfully and courageously as Paul did.

I believe the following illustration describes our Lord and can *persuade us to* **STAND**.

Day 29

STRENGTH
KIND
LOVING
JOYFUL
GIVING
PATIENT
FAITHFUL
COURAGEOUS /CARING/COMPASSIONATE
EVER-PRESENT/ALL-KNOWING/ALMIGHTY
TRUSTWORTHY
COUNSELOR
DELIVERER
REDEEMER
PEACEFUL
MERCIFUL
TRUTHFUL
GRACIOUS
FORGIVING
POWERFUL

STAND   PERSUADED in Whom you **STAND**

Day 30

SATISFIED

John 20:27

"Then He said to Thomas, 'Reach your finger here, and look at my hands; and reach your hand here, and put it into My side. Do not be unbelieving, but believing.'"

I am so thankful to Christ for His grace that covers our unbelief and fear as He did for Thomas.

Tim Wright, a special friend of mine and gifted song writer, has written an anointed song titled, SATISFIED, that reveals the glory Thomas experienced as he extended his faith and touched the side of His Savior.

SATISFIED

Believing is how we will glorify you
By saying amen to all that You do
You get the most glory out of my life
When in You, I am Satisfied!

I am condemned to salvation, a prisoner of hope
You.ve hi-jacked my will, and vanquished my no
You.ve left me with only one choice to believe
In the perfection You've put in me
Well, it's Christ inside of me!

Day 30

> ***I'm drinking the life that flows from Your side***
> ***The joy that You give me will never run dry***
> ***You've spilled out Your love, and I'm open wide***
> ***Eternally I'm satisfied!***

> *Jesus has made us perfectly one*
> *The Feast of the Lamb has already begun*
> *Let the read gospel resound in the Church*
> *As we boast in Your finished work*

> ***I'm drinking the life that flows from Your side***
> ***The joy that You give me will never run dry***
> ***You've spilled out Your love, and I'm open wide***
> ***Eternally I'm satisfied!***

Reread the lyrics in bold. Extend you faith into the wounds He suffered for you. Commune with Christ and drink deep the life that flows from His side.

Drink deep . . . now . . . you can . . . **STAND.**

You have read and prayed through this devotional.

Your mind is renewed with the power of His truth.

You are fixed, focused, prepared, ready and . . . SATISFIED!

Day 30

STRENGTH   is now in you!

Having done ALL to **STAND** . . . **STAND BELIEVING!**

Christ does not say **standing** is easy.

He, who has overcome, just promises you are not alone.

He is with you ALWAYS . . . in ALL things . . .

> *"And Jesus came and spoke to them saying,*
> *'All authority has been given to me in heaven and on earth.*
> *Go therefore and make disciples of all the nations baptizing them*
> *in the name of the Father and the Son and of the Holy Spirit,*
> *teaching them to observe all things that I have commanded you;*
> *and lo, I am with you always even to the end of the age.'"*
> Matthew 28:26–20.

AMEN

ACCESSING SONGS USED IN THIS DEVOTIONAL

Each song used in this Devotional may be accessed on **YouTube** by putting in the name of the Song and the Song Writer.

Hearing the music with the words and the spirit of the song will magnify the significance of each song used in this devotional.

Outrageous Grace
by Godfrey Birtill

* * *

Same Power
by Jeremy Camp

* * *

I Have Decided to Follow Jesus
by various Artists

* * *

Satisfied
by Tim Wright

CPSIA information can be obtained
at www.ICGtesting.com
Printed in the USA
FFOW04n1850040216
21093FF

9 781609 201098